Dear Family and Friends of Young Readers,

Learning to read is one of the most important milestones your child will ever attain. Early reading is hard work, but you can make it easier with Hello Readers.

Just like learning to play a sport or an instrument, learning to read requires many opportunities to work on skills. However, you have to get in the game or experience real music to keep interested and motivated. Hello Readers are carefully structured to provide the right level of text for practice and great stories for experiencing the fun of reading.

Try these activities:

• Reading starts with the alphabet and at the earliest level, you may encourage your child to focus on the sounds of letters in words and sounding out words. With more experienced readers, focus on how words are spelled. Be word watchers!

• Go beyond the book — talk about the story, how it compares with other stories, and what your child likes about it.

• Comprehension — did your child get it? Have your child retell the story or answer questions you may ask about it.

Another thing children learn to do at this age is learn to ride a bike. You put training wheels on to help them in the beginning and guide the bike from behind. Hello Readers help you support your child and then you get to watch them take off as skilled readers.

— Francie Alexander
  Chief Academic Officer,
  Scholastic Education

For Heidi,
our marvelous mariposa, as she spreads
her wings and soars into life.
—C. & P.R.

The authors would like to thank Peter "Korn" Korb,
Betty and Dick, Mary Ann,
and the Welke family—Ann, Daryl, Jaime, and Kate.

To my kids, Wolf and Teal
—M.M.

Library of Congress Cataloging-in-Publication Data available.

ISBN 0-439-43965-5

Text copyright © 2003 by Connie and Peter Roop.
Illustrations copyright © 2003 by Mike Maydak.
All rights reserved.   Published by Scholastic Inc.
SCHOLASTIC, HELLO READER, and associated logos are trademarks and/or registered trademarks of Scholastic Inc.

12 11 10 9 8 7 6 5 4 3 2 1   3 4 5 6 7 8/0

Printed in the U.S.A.
First printing, March 2003

Millions of Monarchs

by Connie and Peter Roop
Illustrated by Mike Maydak

Hello Reader! Science — Level 1

SCHOLASTIC INC.

New York   Toronto   London   Auckland   Sydney
Mexico City   New Delhi   Hong Kong   Buenos Aires

Fall comes.
Leaves change.
One monarch flies south.

She soars high.

She glides low.

She flies to Mexico.

She dips to sip nectar.
More monarchs flutter down
to join her.

The monarchs flit from flower to flower.
The flower nectar powers the monarchs as they fly to Mexico.

Lightning flashes.
Thunder crashes.
The monarchs hide from the storm.

The storm stops.
The migrating monarchs fly high
into the blue sky.

The monarchs ride a gentle breeze
across a lake.
The warm wind carries
them farther south.

Millions of monarchs arrive in Mexico.

All winter, millions of monarchs cluster together.

The morning sun warms the monarchs.
The monarchs soar, glide, dip, and dive.

They drink water
from cool mountain streams.

They sip nectar from bright red flowers.

Spring comes.
Millions of monarchs fly north.

When fall comes again, millions of monarchs will fly south to Mexico.